Animals
of the Frozen South

by Lisa Moore • illustrated by Miro Salazar

Harcourt

Orlando   Boston   Dallas   Chicago   San Diego

Visit *The Learning Site!*
www.harcourtschool.com

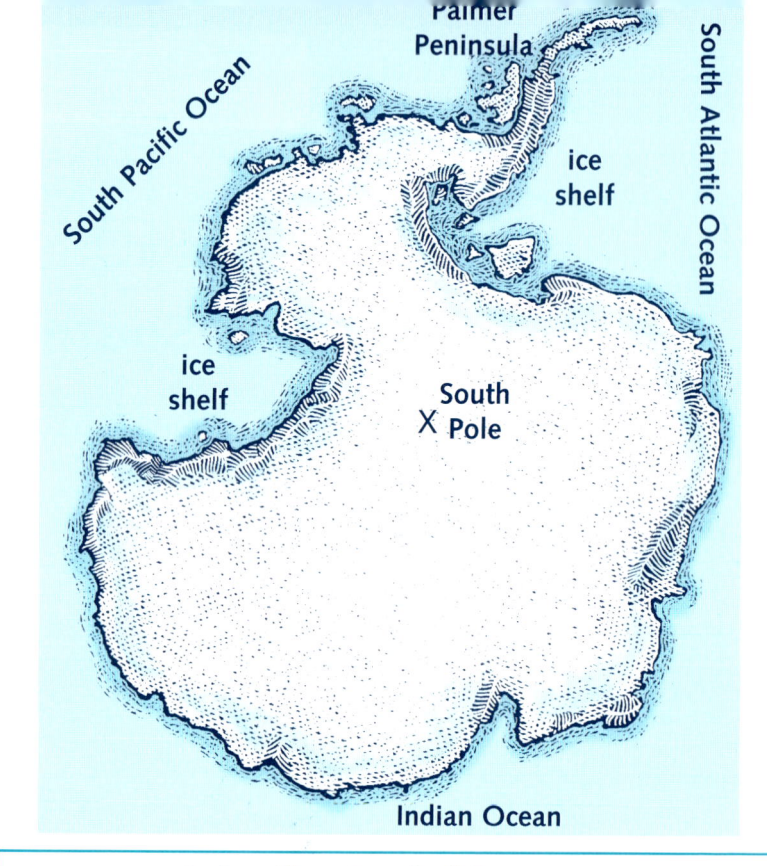

Antarctica: Land of Extremes

Antarctica is the coldest, windiest place on Earth. Layers of ice and snow a mile thick bury most of the continent. Here and there nearly impassable mountains jut through the ice. Stormy seas choked with ice chunks surround the land. In winter (May through September), temperatures drop to –100°F. In summer they can rise to 40°F. Sometimes on the warmest summer days, some of the ice melts—but not much.

Antarctica is a land of extreme light and darkness. Spring approaches in October; days get longer and longer. By November the sun marches around the northern horizon and dips only briefly from sight. By midsummer, in December, days are nearly twenty-three hours long. Winter is the opposite. June seems like a single long night with only a few brief hours of dim glow.

The entire region is home to fewer than seventy species of animals, forty-four of which are insects. No land mammals live there, but several kinds of whales and five kinds of seals inhabit the waters nearby. About a dozen species of birds visit. All Antarctic life is found near the coasts or in the seas. No animals live in the barren interior.

Plants in Antarctica

Most plants in Antarctica are the simplest ones: algae, lichens, and mosses. It's possible that certain lichens in the Antarctic may be Earth's oldest living things. Antarctic mosses are extremely hardy. In the winter they become so dry and brittle from dehydration that they crumble to the touch. With spring's warmth and moisture, they become soft, delicate, life-bearing plants once again.

The three flowering plants native to Antarctica all live on the Palmer Peninsula, which has the continent's mildest climate. Two are species of grasses. The third is a kind of carnation. Scientists suspect that these plants are recent arrivals, probably from South America.

Land Animals

In Antarctica the greatest variety of land animals live among the lichen and mosses of the coastal regions. You might be surprised at what appears on the list: a few mites, ticks, wingless springtails, lice, and flies. Through most of the year, they exist in a frozen state, thawing out only for a brief burst of activity under the direct rays of the summer sun.

The largest known Antarctic land animal—the giant of them all—is a wingless mosquito! It is less than a tenth of an inch long.

Terns

Terns are seabirds related to gulls and famous for their powers of flight. Antarctic terns are big, with wingspans of up to twenty-four inches. To feed, terns soar through the cold, dry air and dive into the sea to catch fish.

Terns nest on the Antarctic coast when spring thaws the land. Their nests are shallow holes in the bare earth. The eggs are a speckled brown or tan color, which matches the ground around the nest, discouraging other animals from raiding it.

Terns' pointed wings carry them through the air swiftly for long distances.

The chicks look like stones. The parents fly to and from the nest, returning with fish for their young.

Two species of terns visit Antarctica over the summer. Antarctic terns breed in Antarctica during the summer months (November to January) and then migrate to warmer seas near South America and South Africa during the winter (May to September). Arctic terns breed near the North Pole in the summer (June to August) and then migrate to the Antarctic to enjoy another summer there (November to January). Clever birds! They migrate a grueling 11,185 miles, a distance unmatched among animals.

In Antarctica the Arctic terns feed at sea on krill and fish before returning north in March. Although they look nearly alike, Arctic and Antarctic terns mate during different times of the year, at opposite poles, and only with others of their own kind.

Penguins

There are eighteen species of penguins on Earth, all living in the Southern Hemisphere. Five species—the chinstrap, gentoo, king, macaroni, and royal penguins—nest in Antarctica but travel to warmer waters during the winter. Two species live exclusively in Antarctica: the Adélie and the emperor penguins.

Penguins' "wings" are stiff flippers. In contrast to all other birds' wings, penguins' wings are designed to push their bodies down, not up. When their wings stop beating, penguins rise to the water's surface. To say that penguins are "flightless" is not entirely correct. They simply "fly" in water rather than air. You could say they spend most of their lives soaring beneath the cold sea.

And Called It Macaroni

Have you ever wondered about the line in "Yankee Doodle" that says, "stuck a feather in his cap and called it macaroni"? In the 1700s, *macaroni* was a slang expression for a gentleman who was so overdressed that he looked silly. The macaroni penguin gets its name from the same expression. It looks like it's wearing feathers in its cap!

Emperor Penguins

At about $3\frac{1}{2}$ feet tall, emperors are the largest penguins. Unlike other penguins, which breed on land in the summer, emperors breed in winter on top of ice shelves. In fact, emperors are wholly oceanic. They are the only birds that may never go on land during their entire lives.

Emperors are famous for the way in which they hatch their young. Usually, the female lays a single, one-pound egg in April or May. After a day, she gives the egg to her male partner to keep warm. The mother leaves for a two-month feast in the open seas. During this time the male penguin keeps the egg in a pocketlike flap of skin on its belly, close to the tops of its feet. The males huddle in groups to protect themselves and their eggs from raging winter storms. The females return just as the eggs are ready to hatch, and then the males leave for the sea.

Emperor Penguin:
order: *Sphenisciformes*
family: *Spheniscidae*
genus: *Aptenodytes*
species: *forsteri*

Adélie Penguins

Much smaller than emperors, Adélies breed in the summer months along the rocky shores. They build their nests of pebbles and stay on them during all kinds of weather. The parents take turns keeping the eggs warm and safe. That way, each parent goes off to swim and fish, sometimes for days, while the other stays with the egg.

Adélies have no natural predators on land, so they have no instinctive fear of humans. In fact, they have gained the reputation of being a little ornery when people are around. Whereas emperor penguins show no interest in humans, Adélies seem to enjoy getting in people's way. Sometimes Antarctic explorers and workers must put up fences to keep Adélies from damaging instruments and other equipment.

Adélies are powerful swimmers. To get away from a leopard seal or a killer whale, they can propel themselves seven feet straight out of the water and onto the safety of an ice floe.

Skuas and Other Birds

The south polar skuas, the pirates of Antarctica, are robber birds. They use their hooked beaks to raid Adélie penguin rookeries, eating eggs and hundreds of chicks. They also attack smaller birds and rob them of their fish.

According to Antarctic explorers, skuas are extremely noisy. One explorer writes that the "raucous screaming never ceased, day or night."

Skuas are greedy garbage collectors that fight over food with each other. They have been known to follow human trails hundreds of miles inland, searching for even the most rancid food left behind by explorers.

Skuas are solitary birds; they do not travel in flocks. They build their nests of sticks and grasses right out in the open on Antarctic shores. Who needs cover when you are always ready to fight?

Other birds of Antarctica include fulmars, cape pigeons, and six kinds of petrels. Petrels may be the most abundant bird on Earth, occurring in vast but unknown numbers on both poles and in all oceans in between.

cape pigeon

petrel

fulmar

skua

leopard seal

Weddell seal

Seals

Leopard seals are the chief enemy of penguins. Ferocious and deadly, they can be ten to twelve feet long. Their strong jaws and sharp teeth make them efficient hunters. These carnivores eat not only penguins but also other seals.

Weddell seals prefer life close to shore. In winter, when their home waters are iced over, they chew a series of breathing holes through the ice. All winter they swim from hole to hole, chomping their way through new ice.

Biggest—and probably ugliest—of all the seals are the elephant seals (sometimes called "sea elephants"). They feed all around the continent of Antarctica. The largest one ever recorded was a male, 21 feet long, that weighed 8,000 pounds. Elephant seals have 15-inch snouts, or "trunks." These trunks usually hang limp, but they inflate when the seals give a hardy roar! One writer observed that elephant seals have watery, bloodshot eyes and runny noses and that their voices are like huge, long belches!

Elephant seals have an unusual diet. One thing they eat is a fish called the ratfish, never found in water less than 50 fathoms (300 feet) deep. Consequently, the seals must often dive far down in the ocean to get their food. Their large, dark, glowing eyes enable them to see even where the light is extremely dim.

elephant seal

Whales

Whales are giants among Antarctic sea animals. There are two kinds of these largest mammals on Earth: those with teeth and those without.

Whales have been living and dying in the Antarctic Ocean for 50 million years. Along whale migration routes the ocean bottom is littered with bones and teeth.

The first travelers to Antarctica saw large numbers of whales. James Ross, who sailed there in 1841, wrote:

> We observed a very great number of the largest-sized black [or right] whales, so tame that they allowed the ship sometimes almost to touch them before they would get out of the way; so that any number of ships might procure a cargo of oil in a short time.

Sadly, it is rare to see a whale in the Antarctic Ocean today. Whalers have reduced most species of whales to small numbers.

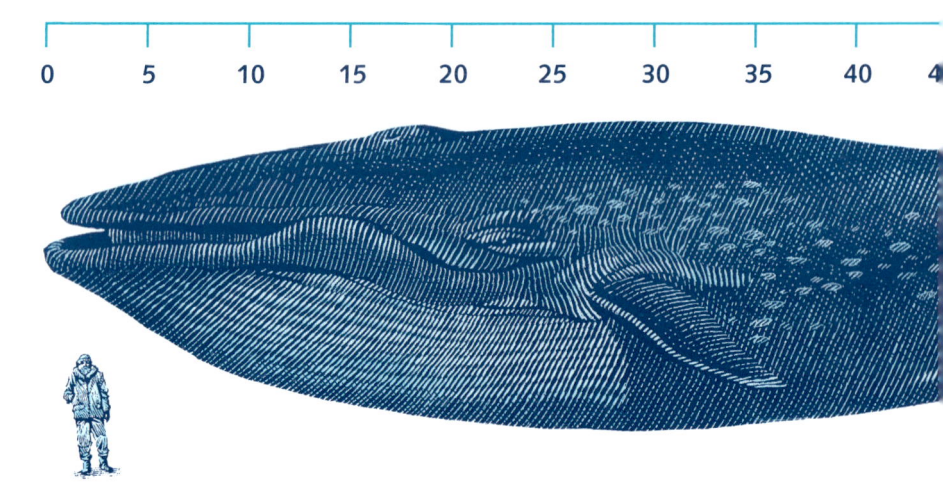

0   5   10   15   20   25   30   35   40   4

Toothless Whales Six species of toothless whales live in Antarctica: humpback, right, minke, fin, sei, and blue whales. All are gigantic and blubbery. At 150 tons and 90 feet long, the blue whale is the largest creature that has ever lived.

Despite their size, the toothless whales are like gentle cows in the Antarctic seas. They graze on krill, tiny sea animals so abundant they can make the water look like soup. Hard skin called baleen fills the mouths of these whales. The baleen hangs in two rows and enables the whales to catch the krill. Baleen is made of the same substance that is in claws and fingernails. By filtering ocean water through this sievelike baleen, a full-grown blue whale can eat 7,900 pounds of krill every day.

On their migratory journeys to warmer waters, many kinds of whales sing. Early sailors found the repeated rhymes and rhythms haunting and human-sounding. One writer described whale songs as "a marvelous series of low whoops and noises like creaking hinges."

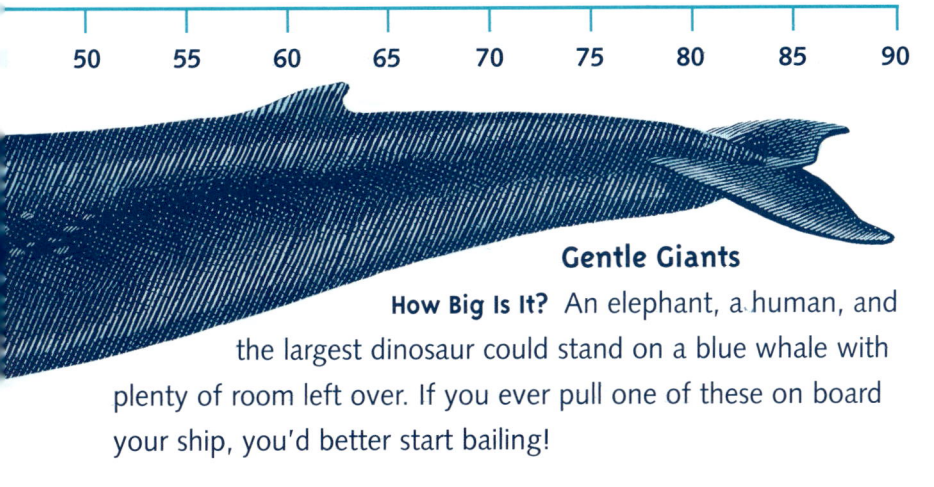

| 50 | 55 | 60 | 65 | 70 | 75 | 80 | 85 | 90 |

Gentle Giants

How Big Is It? An elephant, a human, and the largest dinosaur could stand on a blue whale with plenty of room left over. If you ever pull one of these on board your ship, you'd better start bailing!

orca

The longest recorded humpback song lasted twenty-one hours without a break. The songs change from year to year, and all the whales seem to adopt the new versions.

No one knows for sure why the whales sing, but most scientists believe that males sing to attract females. Also, the songs may serve as beacons to connect whole pods of traveling whales in a net of sound.

Toothed Whales

If the baleen whales are the grazing cows of the southern seas, the toothed whales are the coyotes and lions—the predators that hunt the other animals in the area, sometimes in packs. Five species of toothed whales live in Antarctica: sperm whales, orcas, southern bottlenose whales, long-finned pilot whales, and Layard's beaked whales.

Orcas (also called "killer whales") are intelligent and highly cooperative animals. They form family groups that bond for decades. A large male—weighing up to 15,430 pounds and sporting a dorsal fin about seven feet long—leads each family group.

Sperm whales are the largest of the meat-eating whales. They sometimes dive 1,000 meters or more below the surface to feed on squid. Like the orcas, sperm whales form family groups, but in their case a dominant female—rather than a male—leads each group.

Like the baleen whales, toothed whales bond with each other by sound. Orcas, for example, use whistles, squeaks, and chains of clicks. Unlike the baleen whales, they also use sound to "visualize" their environment. Sound waves bounce back at them and help them locate fish and other objects around them.

Toothed whales are not very fussy eaters. Orcas eat fish, birds, and even mammals, including baleen whales. Remember that a baleen whale might weigh more than 220,450 pounds. It takes a whole pod of orcas, weighing 15,430 pounds each, to kill such a massive prey, but sometimes they do.

sperm whale

The Future of Antarctica's Animals

The 20th century was a perilous time for the animals of Antarctica, mostly due to humans. Because these animals lived for millions of years without humans, they developed no natural fear of humans or of our technology.

Before laws were made to protect the elephant seal, for example, seal hunters killed so many for their oil that they reduced them to near extinction. Similarly, during the 1800s, people killed uncounted millions of penguins to make oil to fuel the Industrial Revolution.

Hunters aren't the only problem. Other human activity can disturb animals enough to interrupt their nesting and breeding. Both Adélie and emperor penguins, for example, nest in huge groups. If an explosion or a helicopter frightens them away, skuas can feast on their eggs. Their entire population can dwindle quickly as a result.

If one animal population is disturbed, others suffer, too. It is up to us—in this century—to determine whether Antarctica's animals will continue to survive.